# JOHN CLARE

# LOVE POEMS

For Chloe

# JOHN CLARE

# LOVE POEMS

Edited by Simon Kövesi

*University of Glasgow and Nottingham Trent University*

M&C Services Company Limited, Bangkok

1999

John Clare (1793-1864)
Love Poems

Published by M&C Services Company Limited
806, 7th floor
Riverhouse Condominium
Ladya Road
Kheang Klongsan
Bangkok
Thailand

M&C Services UK Distribution:
PO Box 3993
Glasgow
Scotland
G51 3YH

First Edition, 1999

Printed by Bell and Bain Limited, Glasgow

ISBN 974 7279 00 2

CONTENTS

## ACKNOWLEDGEMENTS

I would like to say thank you to staff at the following libraries: the British Library; the Northampton Central Library; the Nottingham Trent University's Clifton Campus Library; the Peterborough Museum and Art Gallery; the University of Glasgow Library. Many members of staff and students in the English and Media Studies Department at Nottingham Trent University and in the English Literature Department at the University of Glasgow have been vital in forging my understanding of poetry and editing, and in bolstering my confidence to put theory into practice. The John Clare Society does great things for Clare studies, and long may it continue to do so. Its members are unstintingly supportive and welcoming. My publisher M&C Services instigated *Love Poems*, and I am grateful for the unrelenting assistance it has given me, and for funding my research trips to the above libraries.

Most importantly, I have been lucky to have had the support of terrific friends, family and tutors. I owe a great deal to the advice and encouragement of lots of people, many of whom will not know about this edition at all, but who have been very important to me at some stage along the way. They will know how. Among many others are Christopher Armitage, Paul Chirico, Philip Clarkstone, Richard Cronin, Ben Cowell, Robert Cummings, Brendan Doherty, Timothy Fulford, Michael and Christine Gorman, Bridget Keegan, Rifat Khan, Robert Kirkpatrick, Istvan, Pauline and Sonya Kövesi, Alex Macdonald, Peter Maclean, Dorothy Macmillan, Mark L. Reed, Iain Sim, Melanie Thomson, Sam Veal, Allen White and Simon Wood.

Two people deserve an especial thank you. John Goodridge has been my Ph.D. supervisor for the past few years. His encouragement, support and knowledge of Clare have been invaluable to me.

Finally, I want to thank Chloe Gorman, to whom this selection is dedicated. Chloe taught me all I know about flowers, fields and love.

Simon Kövesi
Glasgow, 1999

# INTRODUCTION

John Clare wrote a great deal of love poetry throughout his life. Although he is now known most famously for poetry which describes and considers the natural world in enchanting detail, he wrote just as many poems which primarily consider love and women. More than most poets of his time, he owed a great deal to the ballad traditions and folk tales which he heard throughout his rural life in Northamptonshire and this continual engagement has been fertile ground for recent Clare criticism. If these traditions surface most clearly in the love poetry, so too do the influences of Clare's literary reading. Clare was an extremely well-read man, and it doesn't take much searching to find traces of other works in his. And it is with similarities and allusions to other writers that we can begin to understand just how individual Clare's poetry is. For example, he owned a translation of Ovid's *The Art of Love,* in which the narrator melodramatically establishes the contradictory emotions of the spurned male lover:

> But, ah! by diff'rent passions I'm oppress'd,
> Fierce love and hate contend within my breast;
> My soul they thus divide, but love, I fear,
> Will prove too strong, and get the mast'ry there;
> I'll strive to hate her, but if that should prove
> A fruitless strife, in spite of me I'll love. (1)

The stark emotional division to which Ovid's speaker exasperatingly concedes, becomes the theme of Clare's 'Love's Story', which perhaps owes as much in its construction to the conceits of the English metaphysical poets as it does to Ovid. It concludes:

> I cannot hate thee,
> Yet my love seems debtor
> To love thee more,
> So hating love thee better.

Like Ovid's speaker, Clare's is unable to prevent himself from loving; he is in debt to the lover, and like all of us who owe others, he half-resents the debt-collector. Representing love as an exchange of emotional capital is a fairly rare conceit in Clare's poetry, but one which significantly dominates the watershed poem *Don Juan* of 1841. Clare often constructs love as something over which the intellect and the will can only exert partial control. In poems such as 'I hid my love', the speaker is almost maddened by secret love, and is forced into a repetitive, irrational ritual of 'kissing flowers'. His love is out of his control; but in his insecure and secret loneliness, flowers provide a sense of community, of rapport, of sympathy. Take for example the following stanza from 'Flowers and Spring'.

> The primrose turned a babbling flower,
> Within its sweet recess:
> I blushed to see their secret bower,
> And turned her name to bless.
> The violet said the eyes were blue,
> I loved, and did they tell me true?

The speaker's tour through the 'flowers' of his life is a tour through the memories of childhood and long-lost loves; the autumnal speaker traces the memory of his own, of his personal, spring. The natural is conceived as an inwardly-reflective space. Each flower is assigned a meaning for the speaker which is only half-uttered; or, as in this stanza, uttered as a question, as doubt, as indeterminate possibility. In her *Flora Domestica* of 1823 Elizabeth Kent wrote that no poets in literary history 'have better understood the language of flowers' (2) than Clare. If 'Flowers and Spring' is evidence to support Kent's praise, it is also a poem which suggests that the language of love was problematic for Clare. By stanza 11 of 'Flowers and Spring' the flowers without a name 'blossomed silent' and 'kept their thoughts unknown'; they are no longer speaking to him of his 'true love' (stanza 9).

In the highly-structured poem 'First Love' the speaker experiences a dramatic and revelatory experience of love; one which threatens to destroy the speaker's understanding of the natural world. His perceiving faculties become somehow altered and distorted in the second stanza:

> And then my blood rushed to my face,
>   And took my eyesight quite away;
> The trees and bushes round the place
>   Seemed midnight at noonday.
> I could not see a single thing
>   Words from my eyes did start –
> They spoke as chords do from the string
>   And blood burnt round my heart.

After the nauseous pallor of the first stanza, life returns to the speaker's face, and in doing so, blinds him. His vision, one might say, is destroyed by the fierce coursing of his blood, and for the first time. The natural world is turned upon its head - time itself is upended - and the speaker just doesn't know where he is. The loss or impairment of his sight has terrified him; he mentions it twice here. The change in metre in the fourth line of this stanza forces us to acknowledge that it is at this centre-point that the speaker is changed: the effects love has wrought on his vision, are wrought in his poetry too. The shorter lines force us along more quickly, as the panicky tempo of the speaker takes effect upon the relating of the narrative. From now on the metre of the poem becomes, roughly, common or ballad metre. The relationship between the vision of the speaker, and his ability to express himself in words, is made more explicit in the lines 'I could not see a single thing / Words from my eyes did start'. It is as if, because *real* sight has been taken away by love, the multiplying sight of the visionary has taken its place; multiplying because he says he 'could not see a *single* thing' (my emphasis); visionary, because words are emerging from his eyes. For the first time he is seeing poetry intermixed with a darkened vision of nature. This 'start' marks the birth of a visionary poet. The experience of love *creates* the poet. The language of love - synonymous here with the language of poetry - is born out of the altered vision of the poet. It is clear that

Clare, in this poem at least, constructs a thoroughly Romantic foundation for the birth of both love and the poet. But instead of the consummation we might expect from a Romantic contemporary like Percy Bysshe Shelley (in *Epipsychidion* for example), Clare's 'First Love' sees the vision of love begin to retreat in the third stanza, and the speaker's unanswered questions take its place. The speaker may now be a poet, seeing with words, but he is not any closer to understanding his love, or indeed, the lover.

The distancing effect of the unanswered questions of 'First Love' evokes the characteristic loneliness of Clare's speakers. Even when he addresses someone directly, it is often to a lover long since past, someone now become strange, displaced or partly forgotten. Even in the happiest of love poems, the desires are frequently expressed as 'I would' or 'I could', rarely as 'I will' or 'I do' or even 'I did'. The conditional tenses suggest impossibility rather than possibility; again, consummation is forced away, into a world in which memory and absence are dominant. These themes cannot be explained away merely by biographical tales of unrequited first love. Clare indeed forged himself a many-faced muse, often calling her 'Mary'; and it is probably true that many poems written for that name are about Mary Joyce, one of his childhood sweethearts. There are many more poems written to Mary than to his real wife Patty (or Martha) Clare. But it is a male literary convention to write not to one's partner, but to an idealised female muse. Far from being evidence of Clare's obsessive delusions, his poems to Mary are clear evidence of his understanding of a male literary tradition. So Dante writes of Beatrice, Robert Herrick of Julia (and many others), Jonathan Swift of Stella and Petrarch of Laura. Of the latter, Byron offers an explanation in Clare's favourite poem *Don Juan:*

> There's doubtless something in domestic doings,
>   Which forms in fact true love's antithesis.
> Romances paint at full length people's wooings,
>   But only give a bust of marriages,
> For no one cares for matrimonial cooings;
>   There's nothing wrong in a connubial kiss.

> Think you, if Laura had been Petrarch's wife,
> He would have written sonnets all his life? (3)

Byron's biting cynicism explains a great deal about Clare's construction of woman. She is rarely the speaker's wife (although this selection contains an exception in 'Mary my Wife'). She is usually young, nubile and rural, but she is rarely a well-developed personality or character (the one exception here is the earthy and humorous portrait in 'My Mary'). She exists in the verse to provide the poet with stimulation, to be his muse; as a result she invariably remains at a distance from him. Any consummation is realised in the creation of verse, not in the conjoining of lovers; rarely in Clare's love poetry is there a sense of reciprocation or unification of love from the woman. Indeed Clare's engagement with femininity is never fully comfortable, as he figures woman in such an abstracted and often objectifying way. There are many late poems, not included here, which establish a pattern of physically-detailed compartmentalisation of woman, rather than a fully-fledged portrait of her. We know little if anything about the real Mary Joyce from Clare's poetry, just as we know nothing of Julia from Robert Herrick's, because the women are figures evoked entirely for male contemplation, not to directly emulate a biographical reality. But his construction of male relationships with females is often contradictory, and depends entirely upon the mood of the male subjects. Even the metaphorical language of love-making changes from poem to poem. For instance, Clare can position the male as a gazing flower (as in 'I'd Gaze My Soul On Thee') or the female as a flower and the male as a promiscuous penetrative bee (see Song: 'Go with your tauntings go!').

Perhaps in essence these love poems are about masculinity, not femininity. They emerge as delicately-structured but frustrated considerations of a man in love. Pathetically, the man is often still alone at the conclusion of the poem, and the woman is but a fled vision, an obscured memory, or a fading flower. But the poems were not written merely for a male audience, nor do they exclude a female readership. After all there are poems included here which have a female speaker, pining for or waiting for an absent male lover.

With a bit of luck, every reader of this book will know what it is like to love, be loved or even to lose love. At their best, these poems are a testament to a poet who was able to explore and express uniquely in verse the varying excitement, contrariness, fragility, secrecy, pain and joy of human love. Such universal themes ensure that Clare's love poetry will always be relevant, and that the language of love will always be worth hearing, even if it is not always understood.

NOTES TO INTRODUCTION

1.) 'Amours', Book III, Elegy XI, *The Art of Love, in Three Books; The Remedy of Love; The Art of Beauty, and Amours, From the Latin of P. N. Ovid,* (London: B. and R. Crosby and Co., 1813), p. 263. See also Catullus, LXXXV, 'I hate and love'.

2.) Elizabeth Kent, *Flora Domestica,* (London: Taylor and Hessey, 1823), p. xxi.

3.) Byron, *Don Juan,* III, viii.

## EDITORIAL NOTE

This selection is designed to be as accessible as possible. Although the poems have been newly-transcribed from original manuscripts, it is not a scholarly edition. Hopefully it will serve as a healthy introduction to John Clare, but of course represents only a tiny fraction of his prodigious output. I have included poems which display some of the range of Clare's poetic adaptability, and have included mainly lyrical verse as a result. I have not included the many long narrative poems, which explore the details of love and life in folk tales; they would require their own edition. The 'Child Harold' manuscripts contain some of Clare's most successful love poetry. With one exception ('I Think of Thee, a Song') I have not included any of these poems because Timothy Chilcott is currently preparing a paperback edition of *The Writings of 1841,* which looks set to become the definitive edition of the work of that crucial year of Clare's output.

The poems are arranged in chronological order, but as so many of Clare's manuscripts are not clearly dated, and so few poems have a date appended to them, other scholarly texts and critical works should be consulted if the reader wishes more detailed historical and biographical information. All Clare-related publications are listed on the internet at the following address: <http://human.ntu.ac.uk/clare>.

All editions of manuscript verse or prose are effectively a re-creation and a new representation of a writer's work. Like most writers of his time, Clare probably expected his editors to make his work presentable and accessible to a wide audience. Clare's written texts are not pure or perfect creations - they are rough and ready for an editor's work. An editor has to be careful to keep as close to Clare's original intentions as possible. It also an editor's job to make his poetry accessible, readable, and presentable. To this end I have only altered manuscript texts for reasons of spelling correction, and light punctuation to help the sense of the poems.

All proper nouns and titles have been capitalised, and where there is a variation in manuscript capitalisation, I have made it consistent, as with 'bee' in 'I hid my love when young while I'. Where the word intended is a standard English word, the spelling has been standardised. If Clare has used a non-standard dialect word, or if the spelling conveys a distinct pronunciation of a word which is different from its standard pronunciation, I have kept his spelling ('childern' for example in 'The Man in Love'). I do keep words which are deliberately spelt to evoke a certain nuance or ambiguity such as 'dye' in 'First Love's Recollections' and 'flye', 'lye' and 'bye' (in 'I hid my love when young while') which are retained for visual-rhyme purposes and Spenserian-like effects.

I have added sparse punctuation to assist comprehension, trying at all times to keep to the metrical flow of the verse. I have mostly avoided any interference with metre. Generally I have not standardised punctuation or spelling where to do so would effect a change in metre, image, dialect, or pronunciation. But with spellings such as 'innoscence' ('The Snowdrop') which have no metrical or aural significance, I have modernised and standardised. Where Clare has elided an '-ed' suffix, I have replaced the 'e'. Possessive and elision apostrophes have been inserted. Where Clare means 'than' by 'then', I have changed the spelling to the latter. All ampersands ('&') have been replaced by 'and'. I have made some corrective tense changes to obvious mistakes, where to do so does not affect metre (e.g. 'ask' to 'asked', in 'The Maiden's Complaint, a Ballad'). I have not corrected verb-forms where the verb does not agree with the subject, (e.g. 'was' in Song: 'Sad was the day...', line 2). Where appropriate, poems have been typeset (i.e. indented according to rhyme-structures) to enhance comprehension of the many different rhyme-schemes and structures Clare uses.

## EARLY RISING

Just at the early peep of dawn,
While brushing through the dewy lawn,
And viewing all the sweets o' morn
That shine at early rising.

Ere the ploughman yoked his team,
Or sun had power to gild the stream,
Or woodlarks 'gan their morning hymn
To hail its early rising.

Wi' modest look and bashful eye,
Artless, innocent and shy,
A lovely maiden passed me by
And charmed my early rising.

Her looks had every power to wound,
Her voice had music in the sound,
When modestly she turned around
To greet my early rising.

Good nature forced the maid to speak
And good behaviour, not to seek,
Gave sweetness to her rosy cheek,
Improved by early rising.

While brambles catched her passing bye,
And her fine leg engaged my eye,
Oh who could paint confusion's dye?
The blush of early rising.

While offering help to climb the stile,
A modest look and winning smile,
(Love beaming in her eyes the while)
Repaid my early rising.

Aside the green hill's steepy brow,
Where shades the oak its darksome bough,
The maiden sat to milk her cow,
The cause of early rising.

The wild rose mingling with the shade
Stung with envy closed to fade,
To see the rose her cheeks displayed,
The fruits of early rising.

The kiss desired – against her will,
To take the milk pail up the hill,
Seemed from resistance sweeter still,
Thrice happy early rising.

And often since aside the grove
I've hie'd to meet the maid I love,
Repeating truths that time shall prove,
Which passed at early rising.
1
May it be mine to spend my days
With her whose beauty claims my praise,
Then joy shall crown my rural lays
And bless my early rising.

## THE SNOWDROP

How beautiful the snowdrop shines
   In purest white arrayed;
Just as when innocence combines
   To form the virtuous maid.

Fair emblem of meek innocence
   Sweet modest flower with thee,
My Chloe's matchless excellence
   Exactly does agree.

And O how charming is her face
   Just like the snowdrop flower,
It gives to every downcast grace
   In love, a double power.

Though every way she darts her eye
   Does kindling flames inspire,
But when her downcast glances flye
   They set my soul on fire.

## A MAIDENEAD

A maidenhead, the virgin's trouble,
Is well compared to a bubble
On a navigable river:
Soon as touched 'tis gone for ever.

## THE POWERFUL SMILE

Dead lies poor Colin murdered by a frown!
   Shot from the strong-armed tower of Chloe's eye;
The cruel dart, did all his hopes uncrown,
   Pierced through his heart, and made him seem to die.

Yet 'spight of this, if o'er his half-shut eyes
   Sweet Chloe deigns a magic smile to fling,
Instant emerging, in a wild suprise,
   From death, to life, fond Lazarus will spring!

## O WORST OF ANGUISH IN THAT ACHING HEART

O worst of anguish in that aching heart,
When fate not choice ordains true love to part;
While truest love with strongest ties does bind
With nature's choice and corresponding mind.

## SONG

Sad was the day when my Willy did leave me,
  Sad was the moments that winged him away,
And oh most distressing and most it did grieve me,
  To witness his looks while I begged him to stay;
It hurt him to think that in vain was I crying
  Which I couldn't help, though I knew it so too;
The trumpets all sounding, the colours all flying
  A soldier my Willy – my Willy must go.

The youths never heeding tomorrow and danger
  Kept laughing and toasting their girls o'er their beer,
But oh my poor Willy just like a lost stranger
  Stood speechless among them half dead as it were;
– He kissed me – 'twas all – not a word when he started,
  And oh in his silence too much I could see:
He knew for a truth and he knew broken-hearted
  That kiss was the last he should ever gie me.

## PATTY OF THE VALE

Where lonesome woodlands close surrounding
  Mark the spot a solitude,
And nature's unchecked scenes abounding
  Form a prospect wild and rude,
A cottage cheers the spot so glooming
  Hid in the hollow of the dale,
Where in youth and beauty blooming
  Lives sweet Patty of the Vale.

Gay as Lambs her cot surrounding
  Sporting wild the shades among,
O'er the hill and bushes bounding
  Artless, innocent and young;
Fresh as blush of morning roses
  Ere the midday suns prevail,
Fair as lily-bud uncloses
  Blooms sweet Patty of the Vale.

Low and humble though her station,
  Dress though mean she's doomed to wear,
Few superiors in the nation
  With her beauty can compare;
What is riches? – not worth naming,
  Though with some they may prevail –
Theirs be choice of wealth proclaiming,
  Mine is Patty of the Vale.

Fools may fancy wealth and fortune
  Join to make a happy pair,
And for such the God importune
  With full many a fruitless prayer;
I their pride and wealth disdaining
  Should my humble hopes prevail,
Happy then without complaining,
  Blessed wi' Patty of the Vale.

## MY MARY

Who lives where beggars rarely speed,
And leads a humdrum life indeed,
As none beside herself would lead?
My Mary.

Who lives where noises never cease,
And what wi' hogs, and ducks, and geese,
Can never have a minute's peace?
My Mary.

Who nearly battled to her chin,
Bangs down the yard through thick and thin,
Nor picks her road, nor cares a pin?
My Mary.

Who, save in Sunday bib and tuck,
Goes daily waddling like a duck,
O'er head and ears in grease and muck?
My Mary.

Unused to pattens or to clogs,
Who takes the swill to serve the hogs,
And steals the milk for cats and dogs?
My Mary.

Who frost and snow, as hard as nails,
Stands out o' doors, and never fails
To wash up things and scour the pails?
My Mary.

Who bustles night and day, in short,
At all catch-jobs of every sort,
And gains her mistress' favour for't?
My Mary.

And who is oft repaid wi' praise,
In doing what her mistress says,
And yielding to her whimmy ways?
My Mary.

For there's none apter, I believe,
At 'creeping up a mistress' sleeve,'
Then this low kindred stump of Eve,
My Mary.

Who when the baby's all beshit,
To please its mamma kisses it,
And vows no rose on earth's so sweet?
My Mary.

But when her mistress is not nigh,
Who swears and wishes it would die,
And pinches it to make it cry?
My Mary.

Oh, rank deceit! what soul could think,
But gently there, revealing ink,
At faults of thine thy friend must wink,
My Mary.

Who, not without a 'spark o' pride,'
Though strong as Grunter's bristly hide,
Doth keep her hair in papers tied?
My Mary.

And mimicking the gentry's way,
Who strives to speak as fine as they,
And mind but every word they say?
My Mary.

And who, though's well bid blind to see,
As her to tell ye A from B,
Thinks herself none o' low degree?
My Mary.

Who prates and runs o'er silly stuff,
And 'mong the boys makes sport enough,
So ugly, silly, droll and rough?
My Mary.

Ugly! muse fo' shame o' thee,
What faults art thou a-going to see,
In one that's 'lotted out to be
My Mary.

But heedless sayings meaneth nought,
Dear Innocent without a fault!
We humbly ask thy pardon for't,
My Mary.

Who low in stature, thick and fat,
Turns brown from going wi'out a hat,
Though not a pin the worse for that?
My Mary.

Who's laughed at too by every whelp,
For failings which they cannot help?
But silly fools will laugh and chelp,
My Mary.

For though in stature mighty small,
And near as thick as thou art tall,
The hand made thee, made us all
My Mary.

And though thy nose hooks down too much,
And prophesies thy chin to touch,
I'm not so nice to look at such,
My Mary.

No, no; about thy nose and chin
It's hooking out, or bending in,
I never heed or care a pin,
My Mary.

And though thy skin is brown and rough,
And formed by nature hard and tough,
All suiteth me, so that's enough,
My Mary.

## EXPECTATION
## A BALLAD

'Tis Saturday night and my shepherd will come
  With a hollow and whistle for me;
Be clear o ye skies take your storm-burthens home
  Let no rain drench our favourite tree;
For I fear by the things that are hopping about
  There's a sign of a storm coming on:
The frog looks as black as the toad that creeps out
  From under its hiding stone.

The cat with her tail runneth round till she reels
  And the pigs race with mouthfuls of hay,
I sigh at the sight – and felt sick over meals
  For I'm lone when my shepherd's away;
When dogs eat the grass it is sure to be rain
  And our dog's in the orchard – e'en now,
The swallows fly low and my heart is in pain,
  While the flies even maddened the cow.

The pigeons have moped on the cote the day long
  And the hens went to bed before noon,
The blackbirds long-still din the woods with their song
  And they look upon showers as a boon;
While they keep their nest dry in the wet hazel bush
  And moisten their black sutty wing,
Did they know but my sorrows they'd quickly be hush:
  Birds to make lovers happy should sing.

And I've often leaned o'er the croft's mossy gate
  To listen birds singing at night,
When I for the sure-footed rover did wait
  And rich was my bosom's delight;

And sweet had it been now I'm waiting anew
  Till the black snail is out from the grain;
But the south's ruddy clouds they have turned black and blue,
  And the blackbirds are singing for rain.

The thrush 'wivy wit wivy wit' t'other night
  Sang aloud in the old sallow bush,
And I called him a pert little urchin outright
  To sing 'heavy wet' – and the thrush
Changed his note in a moment to 'cheer up' and 'cheer',
  And the clouds crept away from the sun,
Till my shepherd he came and when thrushes I hear
  My heart with the music is won.

But the blackbird is rude and insulting and now
  The more the clouds blacken the sky,
The louder he sings from the green hazel bough
  But he may be sad by and by;
For the cowboy is stooping beneath the oak tree
  Whose branches hang down to the ground,
And beating his stick on the bushes to see
  If a bird startles out from the sound.

So silence is safety and bird have a care
  Or your song will your dwelling betray;
For yesterday morning I saw your nest there
  But sung not to fright ye away;
And now the boys near you – well done cunning bird –
  You have ceased and popped out t'other side;
Your nest it is safe, not a leaf has he stirred,
  And I have my shepherd descried.

## SONG

Go with your tauntings go!
Ne'er think to hurt me so!
  I'll scoff at your disdain
Cold though the winter blow;
When hills are free from snow
  It will be spring again.

So go and fare ye well!
Nor think ye'll have to tell
  Of wounded hearts from me,
Locked up in your heart's cell
Mine still at home doth dwell
  In its first liberty.

Bees sip not at one flower,
Spring comes not with one shower,
  Nor shines the sun alone
Upon one favoured hour,
But with unstinted power
  Makes every day his own.

And for my freedom's sake
With such I'll pattern take
  And rove and revel on;
Your gall shall never make
Me honeyed paths forsake
  So prithee get thee gone!

And when my toil is blest
And I find a maid possest
  Of truth that's not in thee,
Like bird that finds its nest,
I'll stop and take my rest
  And love as she loves me.

## SONG

I dreamed of love and thought it sweet
And took the winter for the spring;
A maiden's charms won me to woo
Where beauty's blooms so thick did hing,
That I from thence did fear no blast
To bid young hope's frail bud decay,
Till tenderest words met bitter scorn
And then I wished myself away.

But all too late and such as she
Might well deserve the wisest mind,
For love sure ne'er met one before
So scornful bent, so seeming kind;
For fair as spring, as summer warm,
Her young blood it did seem to flow,
And yet her heart did prove so cold
Love's bud died there and could not flow.

Her face looks open as the day,
And in her lips and in her eyes
Smiles and goodwill do seem to play
That are love's deaths in green disguise;
Her breasts peep from her kerchief folds,
Like sunshine through a parting cloud,
And yet love finds within that bed
Naught but a dead and wintry shroud.

All hopes are gone that wished her mine,
And now her mind I prove and know
I'm glad – and yet methinks those hopes
That then did cheat, did cheer me so;

I almost wish I ne'er had sued,
But still hoped on and still believed,
For it were best to dream of joy
Than thus to wake and be deceived.

## BALLAD

I've often had hours to be meeting the lasses
  And wished that the sun in his setting could stay,
And old creeping time a-dozed over his glasses
  And make lovers' hours at least long as a day;
But when at the even love's presence were greeting
  Swift as the racehorse time seems to spur by,
And when lovers part till the next hour of meeting,
  As slow as a snail creeps, the lagging hours dye.

And I've been wi' many as fair as thee Mary
  And I've kissed full-many a cheek red as thine,
And round as soft bosoms in dresses as airy
  My arm did full-often enraptured entwine;
But never o never such 'lectrified feeling
  Ere throbbed through my heart, be as fair as they be,
When round thy sweet charms my embraces was stealing
  My soul stood spectator in presence of thee.

The mould of an angel gave birth to thee Mary
  And all reason startled away from thy charms,
My senses mixed vapour in summer gales airy
  And thou seemed immortal when rapt in my arms;
And I've met wi' blisses and crosses contrary
  But that happy moment that blessed me wi' thee,
That heaven-crowned swoonings unrivalled my Mary
  Nor can hell be worse than that parting wi' thee.

## BALLAD

Mary fate lent me a moment of pleasure
  Just to insure me in ages of pain,
Just bid me meet thee and wish for the treasure
  To frown back and tell me I wished it in vain;
Just like spring sunshine I met with thee Mary
  That shines for a moment and cloudeth again,
But alas in our love there is one thing contrary
  Fate's clouds of that moment cleared never again.

Mary fond feelings will never forsake me,
  Never again though I'm happy with thee,
Hope paints the cure that enraptured could make me
  Though fate to torment vows it never shall be.
Mary hope whispers some chance in our favour
  That still I may gaze on thy beauties once more,
But fate's bonds are on me, that cruel enslaver,
  And love is not lawful to meet as before.

Mary how sweet when love smiled in thy feature,
  Still though in sadness huge sighs often fell,
Surely those sighs was the instinct of nature,
  Of future forebodings fate cared not to tell;
Mary thy smiles still endear our departure
  Though they do haunt me in gloomy deform,
Like waning sunbeams the clouds follow after
  That just give a glance ere they're lost in the storm.

## BALLAD

O would I were the little bird
  To love without a fear,
I'd up and tell my love a tale
  Might win an angel's ear;
I'd up and tell a tale of truth
  A tale of trouble too,
How I do love – how fain to tell,
  For that I dare not do.

O would I were the golden cage
  And she the little dove,
To wear her on my breast for aye
  A bosom-load of love;
My heart alone her perch should be
  Whereon to nest and woo,
There love my fill and own it all
  For that I dare not do.

O would I were the little flower
  The flower shé favours best,
I'd waste my fragrance all for love
  Upon her bonny breast;
I'd press with joy my snowy bed
  And kiss my pillow too,
And love till death and say I would
  But that I dare not do.

O would I were but any thing
  Than the poor thing I be
A bird or flower or e'en a flye,
  Less fear it owns than me;

’Twill try both lip and bosom where
  My hopes dare never go,
And sing where I must silent mourn
  For what I dare not do.

## BALLAD

Sweet are the blossoms the summer adorning
  Shed in profusion o'er meadow and lea,
Decked with the charms of the dew-sprinkled morning
  Ere the sun's spangles dry blossom and tree;
While as I wander by wood, bank and fountain
  Hushing my cares in a landscape so fine,
Mary selections of blossoms I'm counting
  To trace in their beauty some likeness of thine.

The valley's wild lily where wood channels whimple
  'Neath the rude hazels low-blooming unseen,
They are thy beauty so artless, so simple,
  Their hue thy sweet bosom, love's bedded between;
The warm streaked woodbine that decks the lane's bushes
  The sweet smelling rose the heath's brambles adorn –
These are the paint of thy cheek's maiden blushes
  And modesty's guardian's expressed in the thorn.

Alas my sweet Mary, but memory alarming
  Soon starts at lost moments when once we did meet,
When I pressed that soft bosom so white and so warming,
  And kissed thy cheek's freshness so luscious and sweet;
Soon then from flowers is thy image extinguished,
  Still pleasures past sting my soul as before,
As I turn to that hour when our bliss was extinguished,
  That hour when I left thee to meet thee no more.

## BALLAD

The sun had grown on lessening day
  A table large and round,
And in the distant vapours grey
  Seemed leaning on the ground;
When Mary like a lingering flower
  Did tenderly agree
To stay beyond her milking hour
  And talk awhile with me.

We wandered till the distant town
  Had silenced nearly dumb,
And lessened on the quiet ear
  Small as the beetles hum;
She turned her buckets upside down
  And made us each a seat,
And there we talked the evening brown
  Beneath the rustling wheat.

And while she milked her breathing cows
  I sat beside the streams,
In musing o'er our evening joys
  Like one in pleasant dreams;
The bats and owls to meet the night
  From hollow trees had gone,
And e'en the flowers had shut for sleep
  And still we lingered on.

We mused in rapture side by side
  Our wishes seemed as one,
We talked of time's retreating tide
  And sighed to find it gone;

And we had sighed more deeply still
  O'er all our pleasures past,
Had we but known what now we know,
  That we had met the last.

## TO —— UNDER A CLOUD

Though lowly flower round thee the storm is brewing,
And my once 'rosebuds' opening into ruin,
  When each leaf fades that gave such hopes of blooming
  And sweets must blight that once were so perfuming,
And all despoiled by luckless, amorous Johnny,
Who sung thee once so artless, blythe and bonny;
  Thy beauty form whose songs so often tell on,
  Thy virtues praised so much but 'flesh is failing',
Yet look thou up above thy coming sorrow,
The tempest falls to day and clears tomorrow;
  If wide mouths can't be stopped, why thou must bear em,
  As horns may chance to bud and I mun wear 'em;
If fates condemned us poor it makes no matter:
Bad news no reason were to be no better.

So wi' the all which thee and I inherits –
My many failings and thy injured merits –
  Wi' little left to say on this or t'other,
  I've spoilt thy bloom not as I'd spoil another;
The common weeds of every gazer's freedom
Have nothing left to value or to heed 'em,
  But thou, loved bud, thy every sweet uncurling,
  Where vice's evil eye its darts were hurling,
Thou still hast beauties every fate pervading,
Now sweets are banished and thy flower is fading;
  Thou still hast beauties left I cannot shun,
From scenes that's past my bosom cannot sever:
  When the flower dies and every beauty's done
The withered remnant stem I'll love for ever.

## THE MAN IN LOVE

With folded arms and downward eye
  Behold the lover roam;
I hear his thoughts in every sigh
  And trace his sorrows home;
In vain he bids his feelings die:
  Love owns no living tomb.

His very silence prophesies
  All what he feels within;
The winds reveal his mysteries
  And silence is of kin
To speech in lovelorn sympathies,
  And thus his plaints begin:

I laugh and jest where many are
  To keep my thoughts unknown,
But ah I groan in deep despair
  Whene'er I am alone,
To see where many maidens are,
  I cannot find my own.

I laugh on all with merry whim
  When merry folks are by,
Though trouble palsies every limb
  And care is ever nigh;
And ah when pleasure's lamps grow dim
  I sit alone and sigh.

I sigh to fear the heart estranged
  Of her my soul endears,
I know how other hearts have ranged
  And feel enough for fears;
I read how other hearts have changed
  Until I'm blind with tears.

I roam in beauty's summer zone
  Where woman grows divine,
Where Venus boasts upon her throne
  See how my childern shine;
But ah I see none like my own
  Or her I hope for mine.

They smile upon the glass that shows
  What beauty's face may be,
But smiles that on the mirror glows
  Are lost in vacancy;
And then I think of one and those
  That once where turned on me.

I hear their voice their merry words
  Though music in their flow,
But from their heart's unfeigned regards
  Few hears a sentence flow;
Yet I of woman's love have heard
  And heard one tell me so.

And if of broken faith I mourn
  While she is far away,
My heart can never cease to burn
  With love from day to day;
A holy fire in living urn
  Time cannot burn away.

Though now I wander in her bowers
  Unnoticed and alone,
And dwell amid her sunny hours
  Like to a senseless stone,
Childern are pleased with any flowers
  But love must have its own.

## THE MAIDEN'S COMPLAINT
## A BALLAD

My partners jeer me all the May
  And call me proud and high,
And court her not the boobies say,
  Or bid your heart goodbye;
And all because a silly swain
  Left home and went to sea,
And wrote across the pathless main
  To throw the cause at me;
He never came my heart to woo
And prithee what could Peggy do?

He walked on Sundays by my side
  And talked of fields and flowers,
I spoke again and then he sighed
  And so he did for hours;
He'd praise the kerchief on my breast,
  The ribbons on my hat,
But from such ways who ever guessed
  That there was aught in that;
He never strove my love to woo
I looked – what else could Peggy do?

And then he'd turn his head away
  To get at hedgerow flowers,
And wade for kingcups in the hay
  And so he did for hours;
But ne'er so much as gave me one
  Or asked for one from me;
Can love make language in a stone?
  Or find a speaking tree?
I had not been a stone to woo,
What else could cruel Peggy do?

## NUTTING

Right rosey gleamed the autumn morn,
  Right golden shone the autumn sun,
The mowers swept the bleached corn
  While long their early shades did run;
The leaves were burnt to many hues,
  The hazel nuts were ripe and brown,
My Mary's kindness could but choose
  To pluck them when I bore them down.

The shells her auburn hair did show
  A semblance faint yet beautiful,
She smiled to hear me tell her so
  Till I forgot the nuts to pull;
I looked up on ash and thorn
  For nuts – my wits was all astray,
She laughed so rich that autumn morn,
  All, all but love was wide away.

And soon the day was on its wane
  Ere joy had thought one hour away,
Who could but wish them back again
  When love was so inclined to stay;
She started at each little sound
  The branches made – yet would her eye
Regret the gloom encroaching round,
  That told her night was in the sky.

I helped her through the hedgerow gap
  And thought the very thorns unkind,
As not to part – while in her lap
  She sought the ripest bunch to find;

Then on a hill beneath a tree
  We leamed her nuts – as lover's spells,
She often threw the nuts at me
  And blushed to see me hurd the shells.

Love tokens for an after day,
  Passports a blushing kiss to claim,
Soon went that autumn eve away
  And never more its fellow came;
The west was in a glorious trim
  Of colours mixed in endless thrall,
And on the dark wood's distant rim
  The sun hung like a golden ball.

Right luscious was those nutting bowers,
  Impulses sweet for many a day,
Joy never smiled on sweeter hours
  Or sighed o'er sweeter passed away;
'Twas Mary's smiles and sweet replies
  That gave the sky so sweet a stain,
So bright I never saw him rise
  Nor ever set so sweet again.

## BALLAD

I dreamt not what it was to woo
   And felt my heart secure,
Till Colin dropt a word or two
   Last evening on the moor;
Though wi' no flattering words the while
   His suit he urged to move,
Fond ways informed me with a smile
   How sweet it was to love.

He left the path to let me pass
   The dripping dews to shun,
And walked himself among the grass,
   I deemed it kindly done;
And when his hand was held to me,
   As o'er each stile we went,
I deemed it rude to say him nay,
   And manners to consent.

He saw me to the town and then
   He sighed but kissed me not,
And whispered 'We shall meet again'
   But didn't say for what;
Yet on my breast his cheek had lain
   And though it gently pressed,
It burned my heart and left a pain
   That robs it of its rest.

## OLD FEELINGS

It did delight me – and delights me still
To make a summer seat upon a hill;
Shielded from sun and wind by little bush,
To list the song and not to start the thrush,
Then rested down a pleasant path to roam,
Through fields where peace is never found from home,
And woods where woodbines dangle in the boughs
Daring the boys to reach them – tending cows –
Who often aided by a treacherous stile,
Climb and destroy them in their idle toil,
Dragging them down and spoiling hedgerow bowers,
Singing more loud when they possess the flowers;
And roads where clover bottles swarm full-blown
Both red and white as thick as they were sown,
Round which the bees go buzzing with delight
Following rich joy that's never out of sight
Then mark a clump of sheep and by and by
A brindled cow among the rushes lie;
Now fresh-ploughed lands seen through the gappy lane
Where peeps the spire that beckons home again,
While o'er the wooden brig that sturts surprise
A footstep hastens and a morehen flies,
And then a tripping maiden skips the stiles
Who speaks in blushes and represses smiles,
So sweet, one turns half round to look again,
To see if she be handsome, fair or plain;
And if she be a woman in her mind
She must be fair and though a savage kind,
And thus we turn to praise – who questions why?
Ask thine own heart when beauty passes bye.

## ON SEEING A BEAUTIFUL STATUE

Thou lovely shade of heavenly birth
  Aught else thou cannot be,
The copy of the loves on earth
  Were never types of thee;
Where is the face can looks impart,
  So heavenly born as thine?
Rude nature tamed with studied art,
  O was nothing so divine?

Thou type of beauty's reigning flower,
  To form thee thus was given
A soul that spurned at earthly power
  And grasped the fire of heaven;
Of faded Greece the Goddess still
  Formed from eternity,
T'were hard to deem it heathen-ill
  To worship such as thee.

For love might yet with bended knee
  Urge its promethean prayer,
And worship in its ecstasy
  The soul thought kindles there;
Beauty's the type of heaven above
  Where sinless praise is given,
Nor is it vain for earth to love
  Aught that resembles heaven.

## FIRST LOVE'S RECOLLECTIONS

First love will with the heart remain
  When all its hopes are bye,
As frail rose blossoms still retain
  Their fragrance when they dye;
And joy's first dreams will haunt the mind
  With shadows whence they sprung,
As summer leaves the stems behind
  On which spring's blossoms hung.

Mary I dare not call thee dear
  I've lost that right so long,
Yet once again I vex thine ear
  With memory's idle song;
Had time and change ne'er blotted out
  The love of former days,
Thou wert the last that I should doubt
  Of pleasing with my praise.

When honeyed tokens from each tongue
  Told with what truth we loved,
How rapturous to thy lips I clung
  Whilst nought but smiles reproved;
But now methinks if one kind word
  Were whispered in thine ear,
Thou'dst startle like an untamed bird
  And blush with wilder fear.

How loath to part, how find to meet
  Had we two used to be,
At sunset with what eager feet
  I hastened on to thee;
Scarce nine days passed us ere we met
  In spring nay winter weather,

Now nine years' suns have risen and set
  Nor found us once together.

Thy face was so familiar grown
  Thyself so often nigh,
A moment's memory when alone
  Would bring thee to mine eye;
But now my very dreams forget
  That witching look to trace,
Though there thy beauty lingers yet
  It wears a stranger's face.

I felt a pride to name thy name
  But now that pride hath flown,
My words e'en seem to blush for shame
  That own I love thee on;
I felt I then thy heart did share
  Nor urged a binding vow,
But much I doubt if thou could spare
  One word of kindness now.

Oh what is now my name to thee
  Though once nought seemed so dear,
Perhaps a jest in hours of glee
  To please some idle ear;
And yet like counterfeits with me
  Impressions linger on,
Though all the gilded finery
  That passed for truth is gone.

Ere the world smiled upon my lays
  A sweeter mead was mine,
Thy blushing look of ready praise
  Was raised at every line;

But now methinks thy fervent love
  Is changed to scorn severe,
And songs that other hearts approve
  Seem to discord to thine ear.

When last thy gentle cheek I prest
  And heard thee feign adieu,
I little thought that seeming jest
  Would prove a word so true;
A fate like this hath oft befell
  E'en loftier hopes than ours:
Spring bids full many buds to swell
  That ne'er can grow to flowers.

## FAREWELL AND DEFIANCE TO LOVE

Love and thy vain employs away
  From this too oft-deluded breast,
No longer will I court thy stay
  To be my bosom's teasing guest;
Thou treacherous medicine reckoned pure,
  Thou quackery of the harassed heart,
That kills what thou pretend'st to cure,
  Life's mountebank thou art.

With nostrum vain of boasted powers
  That ta'en a worse disorder breeds,
An asp hid in a group of flowers
  That kills and slays when none perceives;
Thou mock truce to the troubled mind
  Leading it on in sorrow's way,
Freedom that leaves us more confined,
  I bid thee hence away.

Dost taunt and deem my power beyond
  The resolution reason gave,
Tut – falsity hath snapped each bond
  That made me once thy quiet slave,
And made thy snare a spider's thread
  Which e'en my breath can break in twain,
Nor will I be like Samson led
  To trust thy wiles again.

I took thee as my staff to guide
  Me on the road I did pursue,
And when my weakness most relied
  Upon its strength it broke in two;

I took thee as my friendly host
  That council might in dangers show,
But when I needed thee the most
  I found thou wert my foe.

So go thou folly-painted toy
  Thou plaything all display,
I will at least out-brave the boy
  And throw such idle toys away;
Thou dream for folly's idle hour
  Which I have found a dream indeed,
Thou distant-seeming showy flower
  That proves when near a weed.

Go trump thy mystic lotteries
  Elsewhere – veiled 'neath deception's blot
Holding out every draw a prize,
  Where worthless blanks are only got;
And flourish with thy patron dame
  Yclept a goddess and her boy,
That fills the world with empty fame
  And lives in painted joy.

Tempt me no more with rosy cheeks
  Nor daze my reason with bright eyes,
I'm wearied with thy painted freaks
  And sicken at such vanities;
Be roses fine as e'er they will
  They with the meanest fade and dye,
And eyes though thronged with darts to kill
  Are doomed to like mortality.

Feed the young bard that madly sips
  His nectar draughts from folly's flowers,
Bright eyes, fair cheeks and ruby lips,
  Till muses melt to honey showers;

Lure him to thrum thy empty lays
  While flattery listens to the chimes,
Till words themselves grow sick with praise
  And stop for want of rhymes.

Let such be still thy paramours
  And chaunt love's old and idle tune,
Robbing the spring of all her flowers
  And heaven of its stars and moon;
To gild with dazzling similes
  Blind folly's vain and empty lay,
I'm sobered from such fantasies
  So get thee hence away.

Nor bid me sigh for mine own cost
  Nor count it loss for mine annoy,
Nor say my stubbornness hath lost
  A paradise of dainty joy;
I'll not believe thee till I know
  That sober reason turns an ape,
Or acts the harlequin to show
  That cares in every shape.

Heart-aching sighs and grief-wrung tears
  Shame blushes at betrayed distress,
Dissembled smiles and jealous fears
  Are nought but real happiness;
Then will I mourn what now I brave
  And suffer Celia's quirks to be,
Like a poor fate-bewildered slave,
  The rulers of my destiny.

I'll weep and sigh when e'er she wills
  To frown – and when she deigns to smile,
It shall be cure for all my ills
  And foolish still I'll laugh the while;

But till that comes I'll bless the rules
  Experience taught and deem it wise,
To hold thee as the game of fools
  And all thy tricks despise.

Though winter comes dreary
  In frost and in snow,
A sun shall come cheery
  And bid them all go;
The spring it shall greet with
  Its song and its showers,
The summer shall meet with
  Its dancing and flowers.

But alas for the lover
  That's loved not again,
No art can discover
  A cure for the pain;
Full-dark is the token
  Of pleasure's adieu,
The heart that is broken
  No hopes can renew.

The star falls in darkness
  To be no more seen,
And leaves a blank markless
  Where splendour hath been;
On the shore speedy dying
  Nought's seen of the wave,
So the heart for love dying
  Sinks into the grave.

## SONG

O the voice of woman's love,
  What a bosom-stirring word;
Was a sweeter ever uttered,
  Was a dearer ever heard
    Than woman's love?

How it melts upon the ear,
  How it nourishes the heart,
Cold ah cold must his appear
  Who hath never shared a part
    Of woman's love.

'Tis a pleasure to the mourner,
'Tis freedom to the thrall,
The pilgrimage of many
And the resting place of all
    Is woman's love.

'Tis the gem of beauty's birth,
  It competes with joys above,
What were angels upon earth
  If without a woman's love,
    A woman's love.

## BALLAD
## THE BACKWARD SPRING

The day waxes warmer
  The winter's far gone
Then come out my charmer
  And bring summer on;
Thy beauty is gleaming
  So sweet where ye be,
'Tis summer and sunshine
  To be only with thee.

Tardy spring came so loathing
  I thought that the spring
Had took winter's clothing
  But no such a thing;
For the snow 'neath the hedges
  Hath packed up and gone,
And May's little pledges
  For summer comes on.

The flower's on the hawthorn,
  Oak balls on the tree,
And the blackbird is building
  Love's palace in glee;
Then come out my charmer
  And lead summer on,
Where e'er thou art smiling
  Care and winter are gone.

Even snow 'neath my feet
  I could fancy to be
A carpet of daisies;
  The rime on the tree
Would bloom in thy smiling
  And quickly appear

Like blossoms beguiling
  The prime of the year.

The ice on the water
  O I could agree
That winter had changed to
  A palace for thee,
Turning pools into mirrors
  And silence to glee,
Reflecting the image
  Of rapture in thee.

Then come forth my charmer,
  Thy presence can charm
Into summer the winter
  To sunshine the storm;
I can think how delightful
  The prospect would be
In summer or winter
  That blessed me with thee.

But the place of thy absence
  All language is lost,
I cannot imagine
  What pain it would cost;
Though without thee I feel
  Where a desert would be,
And all in thy presence
  Grows Eden with me.

## HAYMAKING

'Tis haytime and the red-complexioned sun
Was scarcely up ere blackbirds had begun
Along the meadow hedges here and there
To sing loud songs to the sweet-smelling air,
Where breath of flowers and grass and happy cow
Fling o'er one's senses streams of fragrance now;
While in some pleasant nook the swain and maid
Lean o'er their rakes and loiter in the shade
Or bend a minute o'er the bridge and throw
Crumbs in their leisure to the fish below;
– Hark at that happy shout and song between –
'Tis pleasure's birthday in her meadow scene;
What joy seems half so rich from pleasure won
As the loud laugh of maidens in the sun.

## MARY LEE

I have traced the valleys fair
In May morning's dewy air
   My bonny Mary Lee;
Wilt thou deign the wreath to wear
   Gathered all for thee?
They are not flowers of pride
For they graced the dingle side,
Yet they grew in heaven's smile
   My gentle Mary Lee;
Can they fear thy frowns the while
   Though offered all by me?

Here's the lily of the vale
That perfumed the morning gale,
   My fairy Mary Lee,
All so spotless and so pale
   Like thine own purity;
And might I make it known
'Tis an emblem of my own
Love – if I dare so name
   My esteem for thee;
Surely flowers can bear no blame
   My bonny Mary Lee.

Here's the violet's modest blue
That 'neath 'awthorns hides from view,
   My gentle Mary Lee,
Would show whose heart is true
   While it think of thee;
Though they choose each lowly spot
The sun disdains them not,

I'm as lowly too indeed,
   My charming Mary Lee,
So I've brought these flowers to plead
   And win a smile from thee.

Here's a wild rose just in bud
Spring's beauty in its hood,
   My bonny Mary Lee;
'Tis the first in all the wood
   I could find for thee;
Though a blush is scarcely seen
Yet it hides its worth within
Like my love for I've no power,
   My angel Mary Lee,
To speak unless the flower
   Can plead excuse for me.

Though they deck no princely halls
In bouquets for glittering balls,
   My gentle Mary Lee,
Richer hues than painted walls
   Might make them dear to thee;
For the blue and laughing sky
Spreads a grander canopy
Than all wealth's golden skill,
   My charming Mary Lee;
Love would make them dearer still
   That offers them to thee.

My wreath of flowers are few
Yet no fairer drank the dew,
   My bonny Mary Lee,
And may seem as trifles too
   Yet not I hope to thee;

Some may boast a richer prize,
Under pride and wealth's disguise,
None a fonder offering bore
  Than mine to thee;
And can true love wish for more?
  Surely not Mary Lee.

## THE ANNIVERSARY
## TO A FLOWER OF THE DESERT

March wakened in wildness
  Or musing in glee
Thy tempest or sunshine
  Is welcome to me;
I found on thy bosom
  A tree's use of spring,
A fairer and dearer
  Than summer could bring.

Ere the throstle had ventured
  A song to the morn,
Or the blackbird to build him
  A nest in the thorn,
On the wild hills of Walkherd
  All withered and bare,
Had Eden existed
  I had thought it was there.

Hope long had been blighted
  Love lingered in chains,
Faith long had been plighted
  To scorn and disdains;
The road it was weary
  That led me along,
With no thought to cheer me
  But the sorrows of song.

I looked to the east, 'twas
  A sunrise in shrouds,
I looked to the west, there
  Was nothing but clouds;

In aching and sorrow
  Hope lost her employ,
She had grief for the morrow
  But no day for joy.

Here a sun burst a cloud where
  I looked for a shower,
Here a spot that seemed desert
  Discovered a flower;
Endowed in youth's glory
  Both blossom and stem,
Was the model of beauty
  And I worshipped the gem.

For my heart it was neuter
  To form and disguise,
Nor like a freebooter
  I looked on the prize;
But with heart that felt friendless
  I wanted a friend,
On a way that seemed endless
  And now met an end.

I loved it and proved it
  And down to this hour
I ne'er saw the beauty
  I found in that flower;
Summer lived in its blossom
  Though winter was bye,
Joy laughed in its bosom
  Though sorrow was nigh.

A palace without it
  A prison would be,
And the cottage that owned it
  Was a palace to me;

My heart it was weary
  I sued as a guest,
Love was all that could cheer me
  And there I had rest.

'Twas the hope most bewitching
  That beauty inspired,
'Twas the joy most enriching
  That fancy admired;
'Twas the bloom of life's fancies
  To garland my brow,
And though sick of romances
  'Tis my bosom's home now.

## A WORLD FOR LOVE

O this world is all too rude for thee with much ado and care,
O this world is but a rude world and hurts a thing so fair;
Was there a nook in which the world had never been to sere,
That world would prove a paradise when thou and love was near,

And there to pluck the blackberry and there to reach the sloe
How joyously and quietly would love thy partner go;
Then rest when weary on a bank where not a grassy blade
Had e'er been bent by trouble's feet and love thy pillow made.

For summer would be evergreen though sloes was in their prime,
And winter smile his frowns to spring in beauty's happy clime,
And months would come and months would go and all in sunny
moods,
And every thing inspired by thee grow beautifully good,

And there to seek a cot unknown to any care and pain,
And there to shut the door alone on singing wind and rain,
Far far away from all the world more rude than rain or wind;
And who could wish a sweeter home or better place to find

Than thus to love and live with thee thou beautiful delight,
Than thus to love and love with thee the summer day and night,
And earth itself where thou had rest would surely smile to see
Herself grow Eden once again possessed of love and thee.

## I THINK OF THEE, A SONG

I think of thee at early day
  And wonder where my love can be,
And when the evening shadows grey
  O how I think of thee.

Along the meadow banks I rove
  And down the flaggy fen,
And hope my first and early love
  To meet thee once again.

I think of thee at dewy morn
  And at the sunny noon,
And walks with thee – now left forlorn
  Beneath the silent moon.

I think of thee, I think of all
  How blessed we both have been;
The sun looks pale upon the wall
  And autumn shuts the scene.

I can't expect to meet thee now
  The winter floods begin,
The wind sighs through the naked bough,
  Sad as my heart within.

I think of thee the seasons through
  In spring when flowers I see;
In winter's lorn and naked view
  I think of only thee.

While life breathes on this earthly ball,
  What e'er my lot may be,
Whether in freedom or in thrall,
  Mary I think of thee.

## SONG

A man may mourn, a man may sigh
Left under man's dominion;
And here, if woman charms his eye,
His freedom leaves a pinion.
They rob him of his liberty
Each hope of being free
Is taken by an evil eye
That feeds on slavery.
O love is but a butterfly
Fond of green fields and the blue sky.

Aye love is fond of liberty!
Green valleys and bright flowers,
Sings seeking honey with the bee
For all the summer hours –
A silent solitary thing
That lives within itself;
You only see his azure wing
That flies from pride and pelf.
O love is like a butterfly
Fond of green fields and purple sky.

This love's a very tender thing
That withering fades from crime,
A singing bee without a sting
A flower in frost and rime;
More tender than the simple maid
Who from seduction flies,
More fair than flowers that love can braid
The birth of paradise.

## FLOWERS AND SPRING

1

And has the spring's all glorious eye,
   No lesson to the mind?
The birds that cleave the golden sky,
   Things to the earth resigned;
Wild flowers that dance to every wind,
Do they no memory leave behind?

2

Aye flowers, the very name of flowers,
   That bloom in wood and glen;
Bring spring to me in winter hours,
   And childhood's dreams again:
The primrose on the woodland lea,
Was more than wealth, and gold to me.

3

The violets by the woodland side,
   As thick as they could snive,
I've talked to them with childish pride,
   As things that were alive.
I find them now in man's distress,
They seem as sweet, yet valueless.

4

The cowslips on the meadow lea,
   How I have run for them:
I looked with wild and childish glee,
   Upon each golden gem:
And when they bowed their heads so shy,
I laughed and thought they danced for joy.

5

And when a man, in early years,
   How sweet they used to come;
And give me tales of smiles and tears,
   And thoughts more dear than home:
Secrets which words would then reprove,
They told the names of early love.

6

The primrose turned a babbling flower,
   Within its sweet recess:
I blushed to see their secret bower,
   And turned her name to bless.
The violet said the eyes were blue,
I loved, and did they tell me true?

7

The cowslips in meadows every where,
   My hearts own thoughts could steal.
I nipped them 'cause they should not hear;
   They smiled, and would reveal.
And o'er each meadow right or wrong;
They sing the name I've worshipped long.

8

The brooks that mirrored clear the sky,
   Full-well I know the spot.
The mouse ear looked with bright blue eye,
   And said forget me not.
And from the brook I turned away,
But heard it many an after day.

9

The kingcup on its slender stalk,
  Within the pasture dell;
Would picture there a pleasant walk,
  With one I loved so well.
They said how sweet at eventide,
'Twould be with true love at thy side.

10

And on the pastures woody knoll,
  I saw the wild bluebell;
On sundays when I used to stroll,
  With her I loved so well.
She culled their flowers the year before,
These bowed, and told the story o'er.

11

And every flower, that had a name,
  Would tell me who was fair,
But those without, as strangers came,
  And blossomed silent there:
I stood to hear but all alone,
They bloomed and kept their thoughts unknown.

12

But seasons now have nought to say,
  The flowers no news to bring;
Alone I live from day to day,
  Flowers seem the bier of spring;
And birds upon the bush, or tree,
All sing a different tale to me.

## STANZAS

1

Black absence hides upon the past,
  I quite forget thy face,
And memory like the angry blast
  Will love's last smile erase;
I try to think of what has been
  But all is blank to me,
And faces pass between
  My early love and thee.

2

I try to trace thy memory now
  And only find thy name,
Those inky lashes on thy brow
  Black hair and eyes the same;
Thy round pale face of snowy dyes
  There's nothing paints thee there,
A darkness comes before my eyes
  For nothing seems so fair.

3

I knew thy name so sweet and young
  'Twas music to my ears,
A silent word upon my tongue
  A hidden thought for years;
Dark hair and lashes swarthy too
  Arched on thy forehead pale,
All else is vanished from my view
  Like voices on the gale.

## LOVE'S STORY

I do not love thee,
So I'll not deceive thee.
I do not love thee,
Yet I'm loth to leave thee.

I do not love thee,
Yet joy's very essence
Comes with thy footstep,
Is complete in thy presence.

I do not love thee,
Yet when gone I sigh,
And think about thee
Till the stars all die.

I do not love thee,
Yet thy bright black eyes
Bring to my heart's soul
Heaven and Paradise.

I do not love thee –
Yet thy handsome ways
Bring me in absence
Almost hopeless days.

I cannot hate thee,
Yet my love seems debtor
To love thee more,
So hating love thee better.

## STANZAS

I had a dream, I thought I spoke,
And still it was a dream;
Another voice the silence broke,
That did so truly seem.
I thought of one in thought's delight,
Nor wished the thought away;
Yet still came on the sleepless night,
And still the weary day.
But sweet that voice hung on my ear,
Like sounds unearthly – everywhere.

It was a voice! It seemed a dream
A waking dream of sleep;
It haunted me, and still I seem
That waking voice to keep.
For there was one I valued more
Than all I'd ever seen;
I wished to keep as heretofore,
And be as I had been.
'Twas heard around – beneath – above –
I wakened, and the voice was love!

## SONG

I hid my love when young while I
Couldn't bear the buzzing of a flye;
I hid my love to my despite
Till I could not bear to look at light;
I dare not gaze upon her face
But left her memory in each place,
Where'ere I saw a wild flower lye
I kissed and bade my love goodbye.

I met her in the greenest dells
Where dewdrops pearl the wood bluebells;
The lost breeze kissed her bright blue eyes,
The bee kissed and went singing bye,
A sun beam found a passage there
A gold chain round her neck so fair,
As secret as the wild bee's song
She lay there all the summer long.

I hid my love in field and town
Till e'en the breeze would knock me down;
The bees seemed singing ballads o'er
The flye's buzz turned a lion's roar
And even silence found a tongue
To haunt me all the summer long:
The riddle nature could not prove
Was nothing else but secret love.

## I LAY ME DOWN WITH THOUGHTS OF THEE

I lay me down with thoughts of thee,
  And dream of thee in sleep,
And when night-dew hangs on the tree
  'Tis beautiful to weep;
'Tis beautiful to see thee pass
  In visions of the night,
With eyes as clear as liquid glass
  And features fair as light.

'Tis beautiful to see thy form
  In the pupil of love's eye,
A woman's shadow soft and warm
  Like an angel from the sky;
With locks of auburn hanging down
  Thy shoulders chaste and white,
Thus fleecy clouds as soft as down
  Hang round the moon at night.

'Tis sweet to see thee vanish past
  In the dark and midnight eye;
I try to clasp the vision fast
  But faster it will fly –
Thou art the soul of midnight thought,
  The life of lonely dreams,
Each night thou'rt in my fancy sought
  Then beautiful all seems.

## FIRST LOVE

1

I ne'er was struck before that hour
  With love so sudden and so sweet;
Her face it bloomed like a sweet flower
  And stole my heart away complete.
My face turned pale as deadly pale
  My legs refused to walk away
And when she looked what could I ail –
  My life and all seemed turned to clay.

2

And then my blood rushed to my face,
  And took my eyesight quite away;
The trees and bushes round the place
  Seemed midnight at noonday.
I could not see a single thing
  Words from my eyes did start –
They spoke as chords do from the string
  And blood burnt round my heart.

3

Are flowers the winter's choice?
  Is love's bed always snow?
She seemed to hear my silent voice
  Not love's appeals to know.
I never saw so sweet a face
  As that I stood before;
My heart has left its dwelling-place
  And can return no more.

## SONG

I saw her crop a rose
Right early in the day,
And I went to kiss the place
Where she broke the rose away;
And I saw the patten rings
Where she o'er the style had gone,
And I love all other things
Her bright eyes look upon.
If she looks upon the hedge, or up the leafing trees,
That whitethorn and the brown oak tree are the dearest things to me.

I have a pleasant hill
Which I sit upon for hours,
Where she cropped some sprigs of thyme
And other little flowers;
And she muttered as she did it
As does beauty in a dream,
And I loved her when she hid it
On her breast so like to cream,
Near the brown mole on her neck – that like a diamond shone
Then my eye was to fire – but my heart was like a stone.

There is a small green place
Where cowslips early curled,
Which on sabbath days I traced,
The dearest in the world;
A little oak spreads o'er it
And throws a shadow round,
A green sward close before it
The greenest ever found;
There is not a woodland nigh, nor is there a green grove,
Yet there the maid stood nigh me and told me all her love.

## TO MARY

1

I sleep with thee and wake with thee
   And yet thou art not there;
I fill my arms with thoughts of thee,
   And press the common air;
Thy eyes are gazing upon mine,
   When thou art out of sight;
My lips are always touching thine,
   At morning noon and night.

2

I think and speak of other things,
   To keep my mind at rest,
But still to thee my memory clings,
   Like love in woman's breast;
I hide it from the world's wide eye,
   And think and speak contrary,
But soft the wind comes from the sky,
   And whispers tales of Mary.

3

The night wind whispers in my ear,
   The moon shines in my face,
A burden still of chilling fear,
   I find in every place;
The breeze is whispering in the bush,
   And the dew fall from the tree,
All sighing on and will not hush,
   Some pleasant tales of thee.

## STANZAS

1

I would not pull a weed away,
  Where she stooped down to see;
I would not pull a branch of May
  Where she admired the tree.

2

Like any child, her quiet mind
  Had love for every thing,
The dangerous of the reptile kind
  She never feared a sting.

3

Upon a worm I would not tread
  Nor even crush the snake,
For she would stroke its spotted head
  And leave it in the brake.

4

I would not wrong the meanest thing
  That she had deigned to touch;
To every flower my eyes would cling
  I loved her smiles so much.

5

I'd love for all she looked upon
  And love for all she did,
The roads looked love where she had gone
  As stranger paths ne'er did.

6

The valley where I saw her gown
  Floating in the wind,
A shower of May-bloom snowing down
  Is pictured on my mind.

7

I saw her by the river sedge
  In green gown floating gay,
The May-bloom winnowed from the hedge
  And whitened all the way.

## I'D GAZE MY SOUL ON THEE

I wish I was the wild woodbine
   Twining round the whitethorn bough;
I wish I was the wild hedge rose
   Upon thy bonny bosom now;
To feel thy thumb and finger nip
   About my twisted stem,
The flowers now touch thy ruby lip,
   To kiss their morning's gem;
My flowers would kiss those lips o' thine
That kissed the dewdrops made divine.

I wish I was what I am not –
   The wild flower nodding on the lea,
To win thy notice on the spot
   And touch thy bosom fond and free;
To touch thy bosom lily-white
To kiss thy shoulders marble bright,
   And in thy bosom dwell;
To be thy heart's one whole delight,
   In thought and sense as well,
My heart's own love could I but be:
A flower I'd gaze my soul on thee.

## SONG

1

I would not feign a single sigh
  Nor weep a single tear for thee,
The soul within these orbs burns dry,
  A desert speaks where love should be.
I would not be a worm to crawl
  A writhing suppliant in thy way,
For love is life, is heaven and all
  The beams of an immortal day.

2

For sighs are idle things, and vain,
  And tears for idiots vainly fall;
I would not kiss thy face again,
  Nor round thy shining slippers crawl.
Love is the honey, not the bee,
  Nor would I turn its sweets to gall
For all the beauty found in thee
  Thy lily neck, rose cheek, and all.

3

I would not feign a single tale
  Thy kindness or thy love to seek,
Nor sigh for Jenny of the vale
  Her ruby smile or rosy cheek.
I would not have a pain to own
  For those dark curls and those bright eyes,
A frowning lip, a heart of stone,
  False love and folly I despise.

## SONG

1

I would not think thee half so fair
   Had I not known that thou excelled
The fairest that were blooming there
   If not the sweetest I beheld.
'Twas so, and more than so to me,
For none could smile so sweet as thee.

2

Calm Sunday noons and moonlight eves
   How beautiful they made thee seem,
The poet such a vision weaves
   As thou wert – seen in angel dreams –
A maiden soon to be a bride
With nought so beautiful beside.

3

We find a flower upon our walk
   In places where we thought none grew,
I saw thy smiles and heard thee talk
   I thought none there as sweet as you.
'Twas so when last we met the while
Could absence e'er forget that smile.

4

I couldn't – and I loved thee more
   When late in hidden thought I met thee
Than e'er I seemed to do before
   I saw where I could not forget thee:
When moonlight walks their views unfurled
And left thee fairest in the world.

5

The best, the fairest, and the dearest –
   The moon looked silent o'er our love
The only witness and the nearest
   To thoughts as angels are above.
I thought of thee and only thee
And felt that such was thine for me.

6

The moonlight walk – the rustic stile
   Where she was richly seated,
Her fine grey eyes owned every smile
   Wi' which true love was treated;
'Twas heaven there and so t'will be
The next time that I meet with thee.

## LOVE

Is love a flower, to bud then bloom,
And give to sunshine its perfume,
Then die and be, as nothing were,
The earth of the succeeding year?
And is it nothing else but earth
Sure it is of holier birth,
Not born to fade and pass away
But like the heaven's eternal ray
Bright, beaming, beautiful and high
As morning in a summer sky,
As sunshine in sweet summer showers,
As colours in the sweetest flowers.
But love's not without shadows born
Nor roses bloom without a thorn.
And love caressing or derided
The flower and leaf is undivided;
Love cannot part or death dissever
The heart truth keeps in love for ever;
Nature cherisheth the flower
And keeps it in a wavering hour
To bloom perennial – no decay
Can ever fade the flower away,
Till earth becomes like heaven above
The paradise of heaven like love.

## MARY

1

It is the evening hour,
How silent all doth lie;
The horned moon she shows her face,
In the river, with the sky;
Just by the path on which we pass
The flaggy lake lies still as glass.

2

Spirit of her I love,
Whispering to me
Stories of sweet visions, as I rove,
Here stop and crop with me
Sweet flowers, that in the still hour grew,
We'll take them home, nor shake off the bright dew.

3

Mary, or sweet spirit of thee,
As the bright sun shines tomorrow,
Thy dark eyes these flowers shall see,
Gathered by me in sorrow,
In the still hour, when my mind was free,
To walk alone – yet wish I walked with thee.

## LOVE

1

Love is a secret,
  Like a bird in a shell,
Like a rose ere it blossom,
  All unseen will it dwell.

2

'Tis the kernel of fruits,
  The germ of all flowers,
The blaze of the diamond,
  The moment of hours.

3

'Tis the star in night's darkness,
  The sky in the river,
The soul in the bosom,
  That wears it for ever.

4

'Tis a word and the dearest,
  Each language has shown,
'Tis a thought the sincerest,
  Any tongue has made known.

5

'Tis the flower of the basket
  All bloom and perfuming,
'Tis the gem of the casket:
  Love, beauty, and woman.

## MARY MY WIFE

1

Mary my wife, the summer is come,
And mellow the note of the summer bees' hum,
And the green fields my Mary are pleasant to see
Where I in the summer went walking with thee;
Still Mary my wife, you may bloom as a flower,
And summer bring to you as pleasant an hour
As it did when we rambled along the old lea,
Yet Mary my wife no more may I see.

2

I would wander all summer and look for wild flowers,
For the summer's the same and as warm are the hours,
As green are the bushes and dark the oak tree
As they were my own Mary when I wandered with thee;
When I see a wild flower or a bright bit of sky,
Sweet Mary my wife then ever seems nigh,
But when I look back the sweet vision is past,
And all my bright fancies have fled with the blast.

## MY SPIRIT LIVES IN SILENT SIGHS

1

My spirit lives in silent sighs
  And gazing upon thee
I hear thy silence make replies
  To every thing but me;
I see thee silent talk to flowers,
  The birds will sing to thee,
And lonely in these lonely hours
  You never talk to me.

2

I never hear thy voice nor know
  Its sound in fancy's ear,
A silent shade where e'er I go
  In beauty hovers near;
Do wild flowers love? I think they do,
  And often stooping down
I hear them talk to shower and dew
  On many a lovely mound.

3

I often see thy fairy form
  In spring's bee-singing hours,
Light stepping on, in fancy warm
  As love among the flowers;
Just as the breeze in sunshine pass
  So maids in summer hours,
They step as not to harm the grass
  Nor tread upon the flowers.

## MY SAILOR LAD

1

O well I mind the morn was chill
  The blackthorn hung i' drops,
And gaily turned the old smock mill
  Though now it almost stops.
In jacket and in trousers blue
  I left my sailor lad,
The ocean keeps him stout and true
  And he was all I had.

2

A slight shower fell from a light sky,
  And pearled each grassy blade,
And half put out the daisy eye
  All gold and silver rayed;
And on each freckled foxglove bell,
  Hung rows and strings o' pearl,
When he last kissed and loved me well
  And called me 'dearest girl'.

3

Three times the common has been white
  With daisies since he went,
The whitethorn blossoming i' light
  The foxglove downward bent;
But he's not yet to me returned
  That gave my bosom joy,
Nor one day have I sat and mourned
  My absent sailor boy.

## REMEMBER DEAR MARY

Remember dear Mary love cannot deceive
Love's truth cannot vary dear Mary believe,
You may hear and believe it, believe it and hear,
Love would not deceive those features so dear;
Believe me dear Mary, to press thy soft hand
Is sweeter than riches in houses and land.

Where I pressed thy soft hand at the dew fall o' eve
I felt the sweet tremble that cannot deceive;
If love you believe in, belief is my love,
As it lived once in Eden ere we fell from above;
To this heartless, this friendless, this desolate earth,
And kept in first love immortality's birth.

'Tis there we last met, I adore thee and love thee,
There's nothing beneath thee, around thee, above thee;
I feel it and know it, I know so and feel,
If your love cannot show it, mine cannot conceal;
But knowing I love, I feel and adore
And the more I behold – only love thee the more.

## SILENT LOVE

1

The dew it trembles on the thorn,
Then vanishes, so love is born;
Young love that speaks in silent thought
Till scorned, then withers and is nought.

2

The pleasure of a single hour
The blooming of a single flower,
The glitter of the morning dew,
Such is young love when it is new.

3

The twitter of the wild bird's wing
The murmur of the bees,
Lays of hay-crickets when they sing,
Or things more frail than these,

4

Such is young love when silence speaks,
Till weary with the joy it seeks;
Then fancy shapes supplies,
Till sick of its own heart it dies.

5

The dewdrop falls at morning hour,
When none are standing by,
And noiseless fades the broken flower,
So love in silence dies.

## SONG

1

The girl I love is flesh and blood
  With face and form of fairest clay,
Straight as the firdale in the wood
  And lovely as a first spring day.

2

The girl I love's a lovely girl
  Bonny and young in every feature
Richer than flowers and strings o' pearl
  A handsome and delightful creature.

3

She's born to grace the realms above
  Where we shall both be seen together,
And sweet and fair the maid I love
  As rose trees are in summer weather.

4

O bonny straight and fair is she
  I wish we both lived close together,
Like as the acorns on the tree
  Or foxglove bells in summer weather.

5

Come to me, love! and let me dwell
  Where oak trees cluster all together,
I'll gaze upon thy blossoms well
  And love, yes love thee then for ever.

6

Her face is like another's face
  As white another's skin may prove,
But no one else could fill the place
  If banished from the maid I love.

## SONG
## THE MAID IN THE MORNING

1

The linnet sat upon its nest
By gales o' morning softly prest,
His green wing and his greener breast
  Was damp wi' dews o' morning;
The dog rose near the oak tree grew
Blushed revelling 'neath a veil o' dew,
A pink's nest to its prickles grew
  Right early i' the morning.

2

The sunshine glittered gold the while
A country maiden clomb the stile,
Her straw hat couldn't hide the smile
  That blushed like early morning;
The lark with feathers all wet through
Looked up above the glassy dew
And to the neighbouring corn field flew
  Fanning the gales o' morning.

3

In every bush was heard a song
Each green grass blade the whole way long,
A silver shining drop there hung,
  The milky dews o' morning;
Where stepping stones stride o'er the brook
The rosy maid I overtook,
How ruddy was her healthy look
  So early in the morning.

4

I took her by the well-burn'd arm
And led her over field and farm
And kissed her o'er cheek so warm
  A rose in early morning;
The spider's lace-work shone like glass
Tied to flowers and cat-tail grass,
The dewdrops bounced before the lass
  Sprinkling the early morning.

5

Her dark curls fanned among the gales
The skylark whistled o'er the vales
I told her love's delightful tales
  Among the dews o' morning;
She cropped a flower, shook off the dew
And on her breast the wild rose grew,
She blushed as fair, as lovely too,
  The living rose o' morning.

## WE'RE LOST AS STRANGERS

The summer rose in love's own hue
  Blushes and blooms so fair and free,
I gaze on thee with looks as true
  Thou look'st on me and vacancy;
Canst thou look here and all forget?
  The place, the time is nothing there –
Then pity man who's so beset,
  And woman e'er was made so fair.

Thy swelling breast is just the same
  As when we met and loved so true,
The enemy sun went down in flame
  And shed her shower of pearly dew;
My arm was o'er thy shoulders thrown
  Thy gentle hand was held in mine,
And now I pass to thee unknown
  Thy eye that brightens only mine.

I guess and know and own it not
  We're lost as strangers, and we pass,
Though there's green places unforgot
  Where love would clasp my bonny lass,
Aye clasp her in the fondest arms
  And hold her like a lump of love,
The same flowers grow in fields and farms
  The same blue sky is arched above.

## VALENTINE – TO MARY

This visionary theme is thine
  From one who loves thee still,
'Tis writ to thee a valentine
  But call it what you will;
No more as wont thy beaming eye
  To violets I compare,
Nor talk about the lily's dye
  To tell thee thou art fair.

The time is past when hope's sweet will
  First linked thy heart with mine,
And the fond muse with simple skill
  Chose thee its valentine;
Though some may yet their power employ
  To wreathe with flowers thy brow,
With me thy love's a withered joy
  With hope thou'rt nothing now.

The all that youth's fond spring esteems
  Its blossoms plucked in May,
Are gone like flowers in summer dreams
  And thoughts of yesterday;
The heavenly dreams of early love
  Youth's spell has broken there,
And left the aching heart to prove
  That earth owns nought so fair.

Spring flowers were fitting hope's young songs
  To grace love's earliest vow,
But withered ones that autumn wrongs
  Are emblems sweetest now;

Their perished blooms that once were green
  Hope's faded tale can tell
Of shadows where a sun hath been
  And suits its memory well.

Then why should I on such a day
  Address a song to thee,
When withered hope hath died away
  And love no more can be?
When blinded fate that still destroys
  Hath rendered all as vain,
And parted from the bosom joys
  'Twill never meet again.

The substance of our joys hath been
  Their flowers have faded long,
But memory keeps the shadow green
  And wakes this idle song;
Then let esteem a welcome prove
  That can't its place resign,
And friendship take the place of love
  To send a valentine.

## SONG

1

Though years may part my love from me
My heart shall true and faithful be;
Though seas again between us roll,
My heart's the needle to the pole,

2

Still pointing true to thee and home,
Wherever I may stay or roam,
The love long-true I had for thee
Like suns that never set shall be.

3

Memory of thee shall still prevail,
Thy voice shall cheer the morning gale,
And should I cross the blue sea-wave,
And should I fill a foreign grave,

4

Thy early smiles and face so fair
In memory's dreams shall bless me there,
Smile in each wave around me spread
And bloom upon my lowly bed;

5

If there it be my lot to sleep
Thy spirit in the dews shall weep,
And in the evening wind shall sigh
And bless me where I lowly lie.

## STANZAS

1

Thy spirit visits me like dew
  That glistens on the flowers,
Falling in the morning blue
  And in the evening hours;
The wild flowers have a feeling
O'er my calm senses stealing
And love's soft dreams revealing
  Seem whispering from the bowers.

2

The foxglove's freckled bells
  That blossom by the wood,
And in the forest dells,
  In the midst of solitude,
There I hear my lover call
Where the whitethorn forms a wall
And the foxglove blossoms tall
  In the tears of eve bedewed.

3

Spirit thou of every place,
  Where love's memories are left
Places green as years of grace,
  Where hope lives of love bereft;
My love lives in these green places
  Where woodbine the whitethorn embraces,
Far from the crowd of worldly places
  Here love's spirit still is left.

## WHEN I WAS YOUNG

When I was young I fell in love, and got but little good on't;
  When she passed, I turned away
At first she would, then wouldn't.
  I wished to speak and then the sigh
Came first and always stopped it;
  Come silence! tell my wishes then,
I thought so, and then dropped it,
  And never tried to speak again.

The path that o'er the cornfield lay
  I met her one day early,
She turned her face another way
  And I walked in the barley;
A lark that moment sought the sky
  Close to her gown or nearly,
Her bright eye looked to see him fly
  And then I loved her dearly.

And turns the rosy cheek to clay,
  'Tis beauty's face in woman's form
That steals the senses all away,
  That rends the bosom like a storm,
Though mild as evening's sober ray;
  The winds they sigh, the dews they weep,
And on the violet's bosom fall:
  First love and truth unriddles all.

## SONG

1

I would not be a withered leaf
   Twirled in an autumn sky,
Mine should not be a life so brief
   To fade and fall and die.

2

Nor would I be a withered flower
   Whose stalk was broke before
The bud showed bloom in spring's young hour,
   Heart sickened at the core.

3

But I would be a happy thought
   With thy sweet sleep to lie,
To live unknown, unseen, unsought,
   And keep my lonely joy.

4

Yes, I would be a ray of light
   In the apple of thy eye,
And watch o'er thee the live long night
   In beauty and in joy.

## AN INVITE TO ETERNITY

1

Wilt thou go with me sweet maid,
Say maiden wilt thou go with me?
Through the valley depths of shade
Of night and dark obscurity,
Where the path hath lost its way,
Where the sun forgets the day,
Where there's nor life nor light to see;
Sweet maiden wilt thou go with me?

2

Where stones will turn to flooding streams,
Where plains will rise like ocean waves,
Where life will fade like visioned dreams,
And mountains darken into caves;
Say maiden wilt thou go with me,
Through this sad non-identity,
Where parents live and are forgot
And sisters live and know us not?

3

Say maiden wilt thou go with me,
In this strange death of life to be,
To live in death and be the same,
Without this life, or home, or name,
At once to be, and not to be,
That was, and is not – yet to see
Things pass like shadows – and the sky
Above, below, around us lie.

4

The land of shadows wilt thou trace
And look – nor know each other's face,
The present mixed with reasons gone
And past and present all as one;
Say maiden can thy life be led
To join the living with the dead?
Then trace thy footsteps on with me,
We're wed to one eternity.

## SONG

1

Where the ash tree weaves
  Shadows over the river,
And the willow's grey leaves
  Shake and quiver –
Meet me and talk, love,
  Down the grasshopper's baulk, love,
And then love for ever.

2

There meet me and talk, love,
  Of love's inward feelings,
Where the clouds look like chalk, love,
  And the huts and the shielings
Lie like love o'er the river,
  Here talk of love's feelings
And love on for ever.

3

Where the bee hums his ballads
  By the river so near it,
Round docks and wild salads
  While all love to hear it,
We'll meet by the river,
  And by old willow pollards
Bid love live for ever.

# MANUSCRIPT SOURCES

All poems have been transcribed and edited from the John Clare Collections at the Northampton Central Library and the Peterborough Museum and Art Gallery, and I am grateful for permission to transcribe from these sources. To keep these notes brief, only the principle manuscript sources are listed below. All other variants and edited versions of the poems, both in manuscript and published forms, are included in John Goodridge's *First-Line Index to the Published & Unpublished Poetry of John Clare,* published on the internet at <http://human.ntu.ac.uk/clare> (Nottingham Trent University, 1998), which also contains a continually updated critical bibliography. Each first line below is followed by a reference to a manuscript source. Northampton manuscripts are indicated by 'Nor', followed by manuscript, volume (in roman numerals where applicable) and first page number. Peterborough manuscript sources are indicated by 'Pet' followed by manuscript and first page number.

A maidenhead, the virgin's trouble, Nor 1, 22
A man may mourn, a man may sigh, Nor 20, I, 250
And has the spring's all glorious eye, Nor 20, I, 45
Black absence hides upon the past, Nor 20, I, 22
Dead lies poor Colin murdered by a frown! Nor 1, 36
First love will with the heart remain, Pet A40, 74
Go with your tauntings go! Pet A40, 62a
How beautiful the snowdrop shines, Nor 1, 67
I do not love thee, Nor 20, I, 220
I dreamed of love and thought it sweet, Pet A40, 98
I dreamt not what it was to woo, Pet A15, 1 & A40, 69a.
I had a dream, I thought I spoke, Nor 20, I, 88
I have traced the valleys fair, Pet A54, 164
I hid my love when young while I, Nor 20, II, 234
I lay me down with thoughts of thee, Nor 20, I, 159
I ne'er was struck before that hour, Nor 20, II, 12 & Pet C3, 23
I saw her crop a rose, Nor 20, I, 287
I sleep with thee and wake with thee, Nor 20, I, 23

INDEX OF TITLES AND FIRST LINES

(Titles in capitals.)